WHITE BULL

White Bull

ELIZABETH HUGHEY

SARABANDE BOOKS

Louisville, KY

Publisher's Cataloging-In-Publication Data
(Prepared by The Donohue Group, Inc.)

Names: Hughey, Elizabeth, author.
Title: White bull / Elizabeth Hughey.
Description: Louisville, KY : Sarabande Books, 2022
Composed entirely of words taken from the letters and
public statements of the notorious segregationist Bull Connor.
Identifiers: ISBN 9781946448828 (paperback) | ISBN 9781946448835 (e-book)
Subjects: LCSH: African Americans—Segregation—Alabama—Birmingham—Poetry.
United States—Race relations—Poetry. | Birmingham (Ala.)—Poetry.
Inheritance and succession—Poetry. | Connor, Eugene, 1897–1973—Influence.
American poetry. | LCGFT: Poetry.
Classification: LCC PS3608.U377 W45 2022 (print) | LCC PS3608.U377 (e-book)
DDC 811/.6—dc23

Cover and interior design by Alban Fischer.
Printed in Canada.
This book is printed on acid-free paper.
Sarabande Books is a nonprofit literary organization.

This project is supported in part by an award from the National Endowment for the Arts.
The Kentucky Arts Council, the state arts agency, supports Sarabande Books with
state tax dollars and federal funding from the National Endowment for the Arts.

For my dad

The poems in this collection are composed entirely of words taken from the letters and public statements of Theophilus Eugene "Bull" Connor, the longtime Commissioner of Public Safety for the city of Birmingham, Alabama. His last years in this position were from 1957 to 1963, the height of the civil rights movement in the South, during which time Connor wielded his power in defense of the city's racial hierarchy.

Contents

Everyone always is repeating the whole of them.

—GERTRUDE STEIN

Introduction

Elizabeth Hughey's poems shred out and repurpose the words of Bull Connor, appropriating them from him as he cruelly appropriated them from us. In turn, we see what those words could have been, what they might have meant. Newly at work, they reclaim a future that could have been, helping us to understand that it is not too late, though many have so clearly and utterly suffered.

The poems play to the loudest of rhetoric, but also to the quietest of experiences, sometimes finding the bridge between them. This is our time in all its complexity and connection: "At night, / we are a family of co-sleepers."

There are insistent pathways here, hard at work plumbing both intimate and public depths, reaching into human layers of concern, despair, and possibility. And out of those complexities they come swinging. To take the infamous Bull Connor's words and set them free as these poems do is to reclaim language in its best-human practice and good spirit. It is a lesson and a reminder.

The hopeful epiphany is in recognizing that language will seem to be but cannot be owned. One version may scare or, if it is slightly altered, lift us. What Hughey has achieved is to take a hurt and make it part of a moving journey. The lines in her poems first center me, then take me in surprising and often unnerving directions, but just a little bit down the road to places plain enough. They are my places and your places—past, present, and future.

White Bull is as timely an offering as can be, a collection that meets our moment, historically and personally. We hear literal weight and ominous language, so neatly phrased, so curiously humanized: "This feels not like grief / but like the word for grief // in a language we don't have, / a word for when two griefs // are carried in the same year / and make another baby grief." Hughey addresses us (and Bull Connor) directly: "When I ask your words / what they did, they'll say nothing." The frustration of good intent, the great weariness of repeatedly reinventing our best sensibilities, seem almost insurmountable: "We've started over / so many times that starting over is all we know." Yet we are offered an ancient consolation, cold or hopeful as it may be: "The day ends / and another grows / in its place."

Thankfully, humor too is present—so clearly in the spirit of human nature. "The way a garden hose tries to be a river, we are trying." Love, laughter, tears, the heat: "Does this afternoon come / in sleeveless?"

I found safe harbor in that declaration . . . *we are trying.*

—*Alberto Ríos, 2020*

I

bank
morale
buy
swimming
in
ghost cars
center
basic
courtesy
bush
touch
time
Dishner
plant
guy
bothered
personally
obtain
forefathers
assign
raise
change
what
everything
triumphantly
swindle
she
charges
violated
strip tease
plague
rights
Clancy
expense
humbly
part
attacks
typewriter
Hall
filed
Methodist
progress
march
fellow
print
secret
headline
being
property
stampede
Lincoln
clock
breach
relentless
talking
stamp
willing
level-headed
cent
maps
political
holes
effect
assassination
station
preservation
remove
nickel
road
weak
minds
black cloud
bids
mayor
signal
Denver
greatly
downstairs
due
am
electricity
graduates
church
unrest
install
fast
classroom
permit
outside
against
Moses
conscientiously
bed
basement
public
Civil War
read
crime
whipped
quarrels
prove
venereal diseases
love
rich
lake

association
lived
dispatcher
bondsmen
bulletin board
wood
library
fixers
Commissioner
hours
steam
couldn't
post
decline
negotiate
basketball
parking
function
candidates
houses
reward
cartoon
haste
bucket
basis
smile
parallel
him
traps
protected
life
half
junior
episode
asinine
constitutional
burr
prize
heartiest
has
contribution
stunk
voice
watchful
kick
evaluating
sensationalism
yellow
demonstrations
foundation
ragged
foreclosure
roll
bunch
stood
sheet metal
sewed
here
football
married
serious
applause
contest
discuss
individually
horror
happy
casualty
cooling
lavish
predictability
matches
say
backbone
earnest
apply
bird
Communist
guarded
suspension
fullest
hospital
truth
solidarity
crazy
Forest Park
parade
transfers
similar
swimming pools
splurge
on
steadily
decision
sleep
promptly
months
firearms
sale
children
midnight
wear
closing
please
intermarried

amend
lawful
shortage
performing
stones
passing
enjoying
struck
Baptist
remote
course
bus
Connally
clerk
tendencies
Soapy Williams
infringe
clubs
kissing
together
rooting
whom
ruling
David
friendly
violation
call
notice
got
aside
robbery
bloodshed
try
lights
museum
been
Prince
sterling
patronage
defamed
evidence
ticket
popular
clinic
eligible
Southside
playgrounds
exposed
colleges
continuance
Shine Cortozzo
nurse
neglected
trainmen
officer
trouble
operation
winked
owned
dare
food
stamps
refrain
acres
delay
whole
swear
large
me
poor
reflection
duties
day
even
tags
adhere
whenever
ordinance
request
fair
railroaded
gear
favorite
cadet
cooperate
smear
Mike
buddy
we've
charge
back
arrange
reveal
pinball
colored
fire hoses
fanatical
absolutely
kind
mass
efforts
telegram
necessary
dozen
sit-ins
ball

felt
floating
crisis
joke
foment
party
ruin
copies
affairs
drastic
parks
play
sergeant
wanted
through
details
race
Homewood
inequitable
within
happen
regret
boy
lunch
every
form
parking lot
Bull
softie
violate
New Year
peaceful
cannot
lost
lots
feather-legged
stores
mighty
toilet
slam
Oliver
suggestion
vast
cotton
clemency
admirable
Alabama State
clear
Fair
red-handed
airline
exchange
air
level
Northern
engender
art
daughter
five
brains
put
pools
boulevard
sister
dose
wing
cleaned
sore
repeating
endorse
jets
Royal Cup
siren
ain't
initial
studied
gratifying
rusty
cities
conspiracy
delta
mountain
grieved
unsettled
riders
feel
blame
hurtful
delegated
hold
gamblers
liquors
render
bellyaching
scouring
community
passenger
unanimous
barbecue
overalls
time
clock
gloves
seen
thoughtful
this

steelworker
can't
health
coal
foreign-owned
full
critical
still
deacon
grass
whether
troubled
foreign
vilification
energies
conventions
tape
film
speaking
age
preach
boasts
Miss
Salvation Army
disappear
lottery
NAACP
previous
minutes
therefore
so
blind
heavy
hung
spotless
deliberate
he
cheap
prevent
fundamental
naming
votes
took
Stevenson
Bud
blocking
had
sit
management
went
Montgomery
ma
numerous
haven't
headache
McBride
consider
Casper
traveling
admit
coming
behooves
Police
enclosure
circulation
attach
grandson
corps
pay
Supreme
character
behind
Wichita
Mountain Brook
diligently
increase
figure
write
problem
rumors
down
big
machine
entangling
spend
instance
cool
don't
Los Angeles
anybody
making
stout
seven
that
waste
hapless
group
like
disaster
nuclear
whipping
cancer
walnut
intermingling

Newhouse
between
after
junk
wish
wall
crooked
herby
facilities
crusade
dodged
hide
integrationist
produce
leaflet
thoroughfare
backs
fire engine
inadequate
night
apology
innings
shortcomings
saddle
homesick
abetted
bench
ability
links
realize
filled
friction
Kansas
general
Bloomer
ear
suspicious
dog pound
right field
splendid
discouraging
jackass
gutted
barn
instructions
repudiate
birth
broken down
propose
pressure
Glen Iris
stooping
purpose
switch
law-passing
person
ready
skillfully
impartially
reformer
to
touchdown
seating
branch
alarmed
caught
Lord
certificate
second
lose
penitentiary
unchecked
freight
Bobby
candy
city
Smyer
Bear Bryant
selfish
Kennedy
congestion
argue
into
epitaph
warrant
October
lenient
forgave
cross
ties
television
left
dismiss
roof
no
em
Bible
eleven
difficult
nevertheless
would
meddler
side
dealers
platform
anxiety
britches

beaten
Democratic
bus station
wall
use
Rogers
discharge
very truly
carefully
standard
recapture
beer
line
automobile
circle
area
rebel
Klansmen
column
guarantee
rattlesnake
taxicab
servile
all good
literature
knowledge
expect
racial
modest
fix
upward
up
injure
crowd
always
inflation
breaking
minority
cap
November
ornamental
gained
filthy
denied
audacity
yesterday
guess
find
Mother's
disgruntled
pasture
Season's Greetings
results
never
man
worth
zone
downtown
Mr. X
salaries
German Shepherd
cold
enforce
tracks
glasses
trust
soldier
Charlotte
epithets
South
sick
fox
parents
remote control
bullets
hotter
Birmingham
merit
juvenile
no
sir
sidewalks
transit
daily
widespread
ex-officio
Weatherly
bonded
heaven
bound
grief
envelope
thread
Blue
bootlegging
freeze
horn
piano
polite
opposite
blink
gentleman
Woolley
pastor
guilty

A Call to Arms

A man will keep trying
to beat the bad energy
out of his father's statue

until the man and the statue
appear to be one mark
on a timeline. Applause

comes from inside the fire
that takes down the stars
and removes the difference

between one thing and
another, between shotguns
and hands. Now we have

just one word
for everything, and we
aren't even saying it.

We are being said
though we can't quite hear
ourselves being said.

The Papers of Bull Connor

Snow falls in the form of a last name
in your letters. It is always snowing
in Alabama in black and white
from your typewriter that sits
on the desk of 1962 with ring marks
and ash. I'll take the words you left
for us and make new colors to wear
on my lips, in *Oxblood*, in *Trampled
Plum*, I will try to kiss the history
out of your words, kiss a cut rose
out of the prosecutor, a summer peach
from the winter impeachment.
I will use only your words, now.
I'll try not to be afraid to kiss
the cottonmouth on the mouth
and the filthy mule, the hot iron.
When I ask your words
what they did, they'll say nothing.
They can't remember
how they were used. They can be
grooms for everyone to marry, again.
They can be teardrop gemstones,
palm leaves, skyrockets. The little
black periods in your letters may grow,
now, to be whole notes, whole nights
released from their blindfolds.

Heave in Heaven

The avenue wakes coated in flower litter,
it is the time in spring when the white trees snow,

an overflowing manhole in the street heaves and spits
red clay water, carrying little flat brides

into the sewer, and an everyday bird covers up
the softer songs of the morning, hiding its half notes

in the boxwoods. Blocks away, a school is sick
with numbers let loose like minutes on vacation time

and I am hoping my sons will not ruin there, that they
will be stain-resistant and mighty in their no-iron pants,

iron hearts. I thought that words said in a particular
order could save all of the children.

I thought I could say the words. I made a list of worries
and a list of thanks, and they were the same.

A day moon is out, like a nick in the sky,
far from full. I like the moon when it's not super,

when it draws back into its place, held up
by telephone wires and evergreens,

when nobody runs out into the street to see it
or calls each other on the phone. That it will be

five o'clock, then six, is too much. At night,
we are a family of co-sleepers, all four in one king,

hot stones under wet leaves, thinking our sons
may fall out of bed straight into a war

and so how softly I pull my children from sleep.
I try to make their pains evenly dosed and time-released.

It never works. I've tried mothering things
that can't be nursed. Snake plants deny me.

I keep believing that I will flower out of some green
branch and be released and carried out over the city,

but I know I am not really a part of the budding
pear trees, I am not even above the ground,

I am down below, and it will have to be the black root
of my own heart that pushes me up out of the dirt

that I've thought, all this time, was the air.

The Belongings

We have to work
with what has been
handed down to us.
We eat off of the words
our grandfathers said.
We sleep in them.
We set our drinks
down upon them.

What were we to do
with the fur stoles
but wear them
to museum balls
on the mildest
of winter nights
heat heavy
on our shoulders
like a burn from the sun
in our great-great-
grandmother's vacation.

We see our reflections
in the sterling set
that we have cleaned
of its meaning.
We could not blame

the knife
for what it divided.
We could not blame
stairs for our falls
or blame the art
for what was praised.

We could not destroy
every thing that was touched.
We still have billfolds,
swimming pools, hangovers,
wingbacks. We had to keep
birdfeeders, cake plates,
neckties and dice.
We kept all of the letters.
We kept all of the trees.

We moved into the names
that were left for us,
and we changed
the locks. Inside
we feel different now,
all sunwink, all meteorite,
but our windows
still look out
over the same city
of unearned suffering
we will not save.

House of Bull

A man sits alone in a house next door
to a man alone in his house next door
to mine. One of these houses is yours.
We walk over your footsteps.
We breathe in the words that you
blew out. It has taken fifty years
for the sounds of the fireworks to wake us
and we never saw the show.
We were children put to bed early.
The teacher said all men go
to the same place to dream
but that is not where we go to see you.
Every window has your face in it.
We can't say which house it is.

Birmingham

The land influenced the concrete to splurge
on air, again, and watercolor figures walked out

of their salaries into the daylight to shake hands
under trees fat with leaves. Theaters, once soldiers

stripped of their stars, were relit, and attorneys
threw ties over their shoulders to eat lunch at

the restaurant on the first floor of the bank
that used to be a hotel that before that was a field,

a placeholder, for what would become our needs.
The way a garden hose tries to be a river, we are trying.

That the sky could be a different color from one day
to the next is enough to throw us off. Today, the sky

is an old stained bedsheet. A line of black ants
on a trash tree tries to look like a sentence. Birds

still seem too nice for us to have here. New leaves
seem impossible. I'm so hot that makeup spreads

around my face like a child's wet painting hung
too soon. I wish that our city had better vandals.

I want to be looking at art instead of having
a new experience. Jets fly over a man-made lake

in a photograph in the museum. We've started over
so many times that starting over is all we know,

making more mud and handprints as we clean.
Birmingham, a name handed down from an older city

coated in black where women had to rub the faces
of their grandfather clocks to know what time

to expect death. If there were hidden caves in our
city, if one overgrown alley led not to another alley

but to a sunlit swimming hole, if from just one window
of the courthouse we could see the small gem

of a blue sea, then we could feel like we are all
on vacation, climbing the ruins of a word

that we could jump off of and touch down into
your coolest parts, where a big fish swims above us,

so great we can put our hands on its white body
and know we have finally settled on the bottom

with the other lost ships and we can see the sun shaking
from above the water, and a black hand
                              releases a black coin.

White Inks

I.

How could we know there was any other way to wake up
than by the unlocking of front doors across a neighborhood,

fathers leaving with combed hair, like ideas out of painted
mouths. But what was being said? Kickstand, lunchbox, carpool,

backboard. The summer heat came up over the mountain,
a trained heat, penned in clay courts. We wore short shorts

over swimsuits over bodies that did not feel right in this day,
something felt off, left open. Afternoons, we roamed the dead air

of ranch houses in the kind of silence that stretches between
voices on the television when the actor is waiting to speak her next

line, but what did she really have to say? It's not that something
was left open, but that something could not be let out,

we could not marry out of our own bodies, and who
should want to? The gardens! The greenest lawns, soft sage under

our feet. Yellow iris, redbud, foxglove, our mothers made
of heavy white blooms. We tried our father's drinks, fishing

for green olives. We could not feel our fingertips.

2.

If there had been a war, there were no ruins. A red mountain
charged between our neighborhood and the city like a bull's shoulders.

Downtown was all yellow notepad and briefcase, office buildings
the color of bodies bled out. The park ponds were dry. Unspecial

city, only pretty at night and from a distance. But we were unspecial,
too, repeatable and expected to repeat. By high school, we were free

to drive around. We picked up Michael and the other Michael
and the new Liz. We parked on the top of the mountain and looked out

over the city, a black pool containing another population of stars.
We felt like we were characters in a movie, but we knew nobody

was watching us, we felt our unimportance like an organ in our
bodies. We looked down upon the city that we said we were from,

where none of us really lived. We could not go there at night.
We would not drive down any numbered streets. All the little lights,

we did not know who they lit up.

Less Than Zero

All matchy-matchy
and too frilly
we were invited
to a tea where
a headache
was served

we said we'd take
the blame with the
amphetamines
we read about
in our library books

we were given a highway
and then billed for it

I said I'd take the debt
for all of us
but I didn't say it
out loud and I haven't
taken any of it

Another Garden Crusade

leaf scatter and lipliner
      men turning on men
lit like lighthouses hidden
      under the bed of
          the beaten black sky
lips press lips before
they know to say *kissing*
      the city is listing
          like a lifted pinball machine
a club beat, a house beat drops
      from out of the skyline
      it gets all brotherly up in here
      and we step two three together
go right cross right together
      left cross left together and turn

Girls of the Lake

We went swimming   in a man's name.
      We put his cold mud   on our arms
            and our faces.   We were clay figures
      on the edge of the water.   No one
could tell us apart.   We did not yet know
      what the lake   was made of.
            We didn't know   what the water had done.

Choke Pear

I have *choke*
and I have *hold*.
Search for *throat*

in Bull's words.
A girl's hands
on a bat as though

it were a rope
that could lift her
out of here.

Those were real feelings
in the outfield,
I tell myself, people

have real feelings
on baseball fields.
They don't feel real

now, though. Find
fat in *fatality*.
Hot, fat

not good at it.
The feelings feel
rained out.

We fight hard
to keep words
from coming out

of our mouths.
Find *sob* in *sober*.
Find *bitter*.

Choke pear
a pear that is
too hard

and bitter to eat.
That fall
ten years later

living back
with my parents
after college

discovering pears
when I would not
let myself eat enough

legs aching from running
but pears were allowed
find *bite* in *prohibited*

nights watching TV
taking the littlest bites
leaving just the wet core

like the backbone
of a small bird
in my hand.

II

grammar
lighted
start
language
stock
valuable
pierce
terminate
breath
promise
holiday
yet
clamp
Rickwood
proud
blow
I
finer
bickering
outlaw
come
led
let
protection
ray
wake
breech
gambling
prohibited
payroll
cast
indecent
racketeers
railroad
harassment
destroy
strife
overpass
throwing
arisen
sober
adopting
reduce
gulf
brilliant
separates
jammed
three-fourths
made
official
earnest
further
sorely
patience
literally
reverse
means
definite
mouth
gifted
heavily
pamper
Merry Christmas
Graves
laugh
Jaycee
shame
clipping
god-fearing
selective
meddle
grade
triumph
look
over
blackie
worst
game
Plantersville
board
ambulance
faults
stop
Belle Meade
former
encourage
beatnik
some
hearings
ministers
dugout
block
opinion
zoning
whiskey
target
curb
vagrant
intermixed
undisputed
box load

stand
standing
fireside
president
normal
unless
at-large
deal
infected
travelers
door
Marsh
studio
confused
portion
disappoint
newsstand
attorney
treasure
underestimating
inclusion
honor
size
morning shift
hunting
how
tellin'
iron
is
dress
estate
became
sit down
defeated
solicit
scattered
distortions
cake
paint
flirt
cliques
spreading
communistic
talk
competed
load
aroused
suburb
know
entirely
outstanding
instrument
copy
core
Sandlin
horror
Sparks
tradition
word
possible
determined
tied
illegal
influence
FBI
building
dollar
wave clubs
Brazil
help
garbage
themselves
frankly
firmness
changes
suggest
sue
Ensley Kiwanis Club
emergencies
ridiculous
wasn't
words
bill
country
courage
national
appearance
dispatches
maybe
trace
fire
excessive
beloved
Cleveland
sovereign
flat
next
ice
electric
toward
recall
imagine
treating
avenue

lunch counter
you
reinstate
pad
segregation
frame
chief
countryman
rectify
placed
lesson
schools
NBC
arbitrarily
heart
mandate
pension
way
Times
problems
revoked
Pacific
friends
professional
notoriety
Smitty
city-owned
handles
collision
Hitler
bitter
Alabama
unfounded
enormous
restraint
if
thank
snow
solemn
favoritism
sea red
a
nice clean cell
goose-egg
presentation
cigaret
titles
dice
told
Lou
kids
county
sock
oil
until
an
volunteers
department
hope
sack
outgunned
sanatorium
rats
may
appreciate
mail
devil
away
too
neck
Walker
calves
postmaster
under
vagrancy
nominees
cell
trampled
white
future
continue
memory
ice
written
utilities
explosions
fly
beauty contest
newspapers
dime
criminals
agitators
fairness
nude
spread
expire
expression
cease
carrying
agitating
commerce
instant
vigorously
Cook
toes

terminal
Loveless
milktoast
seriously
brainstorm
tornado
begun
throats
abolish
lapse
my
bloc
revive
honest
record
crippled
several
saving
hate
needed
mistaken
sewer
ran
responsive
failed
substitute
we're
bygones
mop
shall
killed
kindness
swamped
certainly
female
people
k9
opportunity
golf
beat
vehicle
unconstitutional
personal
governor
bit
choke
post
hoses
Graymont
else
organized
defeatist
corruption
teenage
out
shape
finest
first
tolerated
taking
little
ultimately
manpower
hardened
beacon
bouncer
bounce
Elizabeth
remind
member
fight
apprehension
broadcast
confidence
keenly
rapping
honeymoon
photo
story
rigid
America
long-time
characters
unite
high school
afternoon
saddened
job
promises
glad
middle
Hirohito
better
chamber
traffic death rate
benefits
monkey
virtue
dogs
PTA
send
smoke screen
shoulders
landing
district
peace

advice
high
which
present
citizen
monopolizing
loose
reoccurring
luck
answer
mph
scared
fun
personnel
vicinity
pat on the back
elsewhere
stolen
express
image
water works
long
enemies
colleagues
cents
God
unconditional
concrete
tests
vain
oscillating
nobody
racker
announcer
ruckus
attempt
sheet
move
representative
decent
centers
quit
introduce
printed
card
petticoats
substantial
refuse
strictly
beauty
scrap
bottom
came
coast
brought
pass
return
reported
foot
mention
by
meddles
dislike
hell
river
company
weeks
slor
challenge
worthy
fortunate
understood
thoughts
experience
stay out
flattering
sympathy
Eastern
attention
along
willow
serve
instill
races
tell
taxes
carriers
believe
grounded
yes
rule-making
sporting events
black
Monday
truly
think
letter
fraction
legion
assured
indebted
shotguns
owe
aid

note
support
sporting
failure
elect
water
showdown
bar
campaigns
grove
patient
mudslinging
assurance
whatever
more
grateful
underfoot
Birmingham
Oriental Iron
Company
collectively
progressive
hook
utmost
billfold
roaming
malicious
groom
traffic
pull
pattern
fingerprints
social
different
banner
first
base
shameful
underage
two
project
although
play
flag
congratulations
ramifications
coffee
its
who
saying
proceedings
abiding
of
soft drinks
Gertrude
land
fence
damage
resign
fault-finding
have
praise
elevators
quick
income
tension
slapped
felony
maintained
Westfield
war
graft
safety
Lamb Bone
Restaurant
aluminum
books
leave
understand
fence-straddler
insisted
burn
watchman
watching
crossings
began
trucks
body
contrary
ordinarily
bicycle
predict
leg
nail
produced
one hundred
somebody
great
movie
cockeyed
upside down
bombings
minimum
take
combined

consolation
he'll
United
given
contacted
revolutionize
slander
cost
your
openly
torch
strive
speed
sell
myself
gubernatorial
solemnly
legally
profoundly
terrible
flowers
chaos
anyhow
home
were
commending
press
see
debt
difficulties
waged
operate
deadest
follow
clergy
hard-down
north
immature
young
Dick
encouragement
defense
court
embarrass
controlled
vandalism
knives
message
clay
fruit
findings
naturally
paratroopers
didn't
mixed
gas
poking
affected
children's
tissue
agitator
servants
hearse
exterminators
segregate
daylight citizen
January
hand
ding
dong
mutual
stick
strong
study
Oxmoor
heard
low
appoint
firemen
helpless
politically
Abe
swan song
beer garden
traffic lights
matinee
squabbling
Legion Field
filling station
fund
bags
buggy
Tide
pipe
oak
ridge
Pine
Castle
Magnolia
December
Mildred
bright
Egypt
Blanche

Bull Becomes a Leaf

With your letters
I make a riverbank
and lie down in
the cool grasses,
black flies studding
the white sky
like commas freed
from a page,
waiting for words
to separate.

There is no river here
but there is a brook
rust-colored
and unraveling from
a tiny kingdom
made of newspapers
and clipped lawns
and the sounds of ice
in drink glasses
basketballs
bouncing
in driveways.

I'll let you
be a leaf

that falls into
this water
and floats into
the past like a black
fly down the black
throat of the blackest
fish.

The day ends
and another grows
in its place.
I know you are not
this day, but I also
know that you are.

I Became a Postcard of Myself

All dabbling, all peach bud,
I was a pasture, once,
too, saddle-stamped,
milk-legged, following
my fathers following
my fathers' fathers,
staying as dog as I could be
until I felt footsteps
in the chambers of my heart.
Then, feathers happened, air-
damned. *Go long!* they said,
and I went.

Laugh Track

when we took off
two cities grew
together down below

the way my hand
fell onto your hand
and made a word

written over
the same word

what we thought to be
an aircraft turned out
to be a theater

the sign that said
applause
was left on all night

our hands are on fire

The Davids

We were pennies dropped
from separate jets
landing in the same glass.

These are the redwoods
we drove through
on the edge of the country

as far as we could get
and still feel attached
to our mothers, grass hills

the color of light beer,
this is where I waited
for the bus in my headphones

and cords, that's the trail
where I ran on Saturdays
passing the same black

comb pressed into the sand.
The first time I saw the comb
I was thinking about David

and then every time I passed it
I thought about David
and then the other David.

I want to show the redwoods
how happy I am now.
They make their own rain.

This is where I heard
for the first time, *He couldn't*
find his way out of a wet paper bag

on the twenty-second floor
of the Bank of America building.
I sent my boss to the wrong city

in Texas for a meeting. I could
not find my way out of my own
name. In front of that building

there is a work of art made
of black rock, the Banker's Heart,
it pulls down the sky

between city buildings.
Nobody could pick him up.
I come back here to run

out of my body, again. Two
Davids. One alive, expecting
a son, and one gone so long

I don't remember where I saw him.

The Missing

We wake into a new time zone
when everything black has already left

and the leaves have received
their threaded details, there is no place

in this morning to kiss
when there isn't even a morning

anymore, so bright, this lunchtime,
clean plates shining on us like headlights

from the table, turn it all off, please,
draw sunglasses over our eyes.

This feels not like grief
but like the word for grief

in a language we don't have,
a word for when two griefs

are carried in the same year
and make another baby grief.

I don't miss the way things were,
yellow flower with lipstick

on your teeth, I miss the way
I was when I thought of what

today would be like, sitting nearly
a year away from the last time

I saw you, safe in my uniform,
hair repeating the same word, *bun*.

Forever hopeful, I signed my letters
with a dog sawing the day into yesterdays

at my feet. I call out what is supposed to be
a name, but is a whole body of children,

all my griefs so small and washable,
the great grief still out there, snowballing,

or has it been divided and delivered
to me in daily papers, in mailboxes full

of bad timing, in little screens lit
with actors kissing actors, I want them

to really love each other, and by
each other, I mean me.

I Was Misty

I didn't yet know that I was an evergreen.
I kept trying to change colors,
following the songs of copiers
and elevators not to the mist of the Pacific
but to the third-floor conference room
where it was always somebody's birthday
and the woman who cut the cake
never ate the cake. She was going through
a divorce. I accidentally threw away
her name. I threw away all of their names
except for two men, partners in losing.
I ate the cake. I ate everything
out of everyone's drawers. I did not know
how to say no thank you. I did not
know how to say I don't love you.
I thought if I repeated a word enough
it would change meanings. I said I love you
to anything, to the starfish on black sand,
I said it the most to the ones I did not love,
but they felt it anyway and I wonder if they are
feeling it now the way I am still not feeling it now.

Bull in Office

I don't like how black-and-white
you make this day, the morning
the color of old newsprint again.

Let me collect the paper clips
from your desk drawers and construct
a suspension bridge from your desk

to mine. We need a river.
Those men at the park would fish
out of a toilet if they had to.

I want the sound of petticoats
to fill in for the trains
and these itchy birds.

I don't have room for you
in any of my drawers.
The steel factories

made the city look like a war zone.
Anything white came home
black. Want me to put on these

goggles and sit in this jet
in the Museum of Flight
and try to get you to the heaven

you believed in? The petticoats have to be
colorful. I'm so sick of the white ones
I've been wearing under my skin.

Bricking Up the Windows

Laced into the afternoon
a repurposed belle
dress that keeps
everyone at a long
distance, I keep running
into the walls, locked
inside my gemstone
that cuts the daylight
into twenty-four
small bites
to be counted
until it is time
for the next bite.
It is time!
I am so unfull.
The train passing
becomes the bell
reminding me
that my suffering
is when pleasure
is missing
my pain level
is the face
drawn with a line
for a mouth
the line is the sign

for taking things
away but that is just
the way I smile.
That line on that face
    is my smile.

Stop Breathing

It is filthy but imagines itself to be clean, it will be clean, it is made of
  stone, it has no cracks down
which crumbs, it is dirty, it is filthy, it is a foul place, but if you say it is
  a heaven

it will be a heaven one day in someone else's mind in someone else's
  apartment in someone else's
television over the radio it is awful but say it is right, it is bleeding, it is
  all blood,

it will not come out, it is damned, but imagine it is soft, loved, wanted,
  birthed, it is terminal,
like a terminal bud, which means it is green, it is responsible for new
  growth, wouldn't that be

lovely, even though it is ugly, infected, sickening, quiet, it is a painting of
  something ugly
and that makes it pretty enough, it was imagined to be pretty one day, it
  has grown on you,

it has grown on us, it is growing, choking, but we can breathe, there is
  always room for breath,
it will breathe again, it will climb softly over you in the night, while you
  are dreaming,

it will be holy when you think it to be holy, a moral, it will come to you
in a story,
a library book, it is closed now, cut off, blackened, it is charred, but
imagine it to return

unburned, fattened, it is asking to be eaten, it is begging to be thought,
it is begging, it is poor,
impoverished, desperate, it almost killed itself but it imagined itself to
keep living and it lives

Song for the Egg Filled with Nude Hose

I have called a dress white
when it was bone, gulf sand
baby teeth, dirty rice. I have

longed to be worn. I have
wanted the plum to want me
to eat it. I just want a plum

to be pleased. I wish to please
every black fly I kill. I will please
pleasure until I am loved
                    by love.

A Promise for the Egg Filled with Cotton Balls

I drink down a little round white word
and wait for the unnamable ghosts
to leave my body, my body a nest
made of the finest cement.
I am asked in waiting rooms,
Is it a yellowthroat or a redwing?
It is a cowbird, I must answer,
it's a bullbird. Still, I will raise
any word I have been given with its
wide-open fig-red mouth.
There is always enough,
I lie, I can be a fraction of a mother.
I can be halved and halved again, the last
morning star floating in steamed milk,
a little bite of me will always be left
for you and you and you and you and you.

Bullflower

I know many of the names of the flowers in your letters, flowers so sick
with explosives that they blew the words off the street signs.

I wrote thank you notes to flowers with a trace of gunmetal on their pretty
parts. Flowers make great architects, now, flowers turned judges, artists,
    a field

of attorneys, manflowers, bullflower. This morning, I found my son,
    Angus,
in your letters. There have been so many Williams, too, his father

and his grandfather. There was no name clean enough for us
to give to our son. I was looking for the word *plate* in your files,

even though I have plenty of words to clean. I have manpower.
I have all of Nature. I can make a tornado out of baby's breath.

Today, I also found a loveless flower who beat a man in your files,
Lieutenant Loveless. Let's not look him up, again. Let's make Loveless

lay down with the man he beat, change blood into soap, and concrete
into a king sheet. I was thinking of the plates we were given as gifts

so fine that we would not eat off of them for the first ten years of
    marriage.
I don't remember why we picked them. Let's put Loveless and his lover

on the shore of a lake, perfectly round, the water holding still the
  white sky,
a fallen moon, before a thrown rock breaks the water like a plate across
  a knee.

Matinee

On a cold spring afternoon, I force my sons out
into the rain. I have not minded stickiness

or messiness. I have practiced being clean
in muddy water. A half-eaten peach is the color

of tea and the yellow windows on the alleys
of Los Angeles down which I am not walking,

all rosemary, all cut roses. If this day were to be
watched on a screen it could be longed for,

March rains, train sounds, tree buds, stone walls,
unruly grass that grew back without being asked

and a mother in the center of it all, wanting this whole
life and another one on top of it, wishing Montana

would lie on top of Alabama, and a garden
from New England would spring up in the south.

Tonight, the wet sidewalk serves up sheet pans
of streetlight, and a chain-link fence holds a parking lot

of an apartment building like an empty gift.
My problem is that the magnolias, the streetlights,

and the rain are not an audience. They do not
give me the award for best pedestrian. I love

nonliving things and they do not love me back.
For this I will sit in front of the fireplace popping

like an old record and let tears wet my cheeks,
and the fire will not be watching. So, you really

don't have a problem, the fire will not say.

The Still Life

I can't breathe out of this picture of a window.
When exactly does the morning end? Today,
I am thankful for five things, but I only have
one of them. It's lunch. I want lunch to last
until bedtime. I need a metal detector
to help me find my car. Can you make the sky
look less hot? Does this afternoon come
in sleeveless? If I could keep just one minute,
I would not keep this one. What part
of the playground speaks to you today?
None of it? The sky is running out of ink.
We have monkey bars and three more minutes
before I must figure out how to type us home.

Say, Speak to Someone

Try not to rob me
said the mother
to the man
and the man said
say please
so the mother
said please
and gave him all
her nothings
and the parking lot
felt full
and the audience
sat in their cars
and sobbed for the ones
who had no cars.

All That Is Holding Us Up

is a black line someone has drawn below our shoes.
What is all of this white space where things used to be?

The way the trees keep raining just after the rain,
all the clouds we have inside of us are clouding

up above and now, look. A child has put black stickers
where the birds should be. And it was my child.

He will not write his name. He makes an *N*
like he's climbing up a mountain and won't come down.

He's got the *I*. *C* might happen. Then comes the little *h*
that flees to the edge of the paper. Don't worry about the birds.

We can make more. All it takes to make a bird is a *W*
and with more *w*'s you can make waves.

The line across the paper, he says, is a lake, now.
                    You can color yourself in and swim.

A Beclouding

Sun, I shouldn't be using you
again today and buds, garden,
bush, tree, green leaf, cloud,
I have to put you down
I know I have more birdsong
but I should stop using birds
they need to be more municipal
they should all be elected
to their branches
I should be walking down
to the federal courthouse
but not in short sleeves
not to pick what grows
on the banks of the train tracks
no more blooms
I've never known what that factory
makes other than white clouds
that's it for clouds, now,
I promise, I will put something
in jail other than fireflies
and dog yaps. I will enforce
some real laws, I will ask only
numbers what I can feel
I feel like some zeros
are missing from my name
I feel like I weigh one hundred

and thirty-five hours, a mutual fund
sounds like something good
for all of us, let us pool our money
and invest in something but not
Sea World. Have you seen *Blackfish*?

III

persist
program
right
memories
occasions
lengthy
streetcars
weak-kneed
before
belong
favor
stretch
seek
girls
sickening
free
face
bus
terminal
invite
floor-man
conference
satisfactory
none
step
skating
water
frills
Vanderbilt
car
Palm Leaf Hotel
inspector
numbers
kept
insert
goggle-eyed
holiday card
song
new
harmony
particulars
idea
permitted
good
son
fired
slue
unparalleled
vigor
correct
total
New Orleans
laws
men
New York City
stranger
real estate
revolving
liable
boycott
void
rotten
eliminate
lie
direct
hurry
assisted
string
however
must
hired
those
trespassing
Uncle
apartment
bonus
courtesies
vacation
Raines
bad
summer
endorsement
commandment
table
utility
face-saving
another
things
noise
offering
scarce
be
conviction
spare
including
ask
reimburse
reciprocate
height
you're
amphetamines
taxpayers
register
devote
aircraft
tunnel

provided
enlist
obscene
degree
anonymous
meteorite
financial
miles
customary
walking
so-called
protect
seaboard
voiced
red
cloud
instituted
remarks
brotherhood
active
Michael
set
tranquility
dud
chin
slot machines
claimed
sleeves
world
accident
adjacent
guided
sorry
knee
I'm
regular
writer
nerve
repugnant
brown
becoming
crucified
magazine
interest
bitten
win
Shuttlesworth
rest
lead
manhood
gymnasium
rampant
street
signs
golly
sounding
separates
power
jail
suds
office
broom
close
ideals
pick
brick
penitentiary
counter
lot
at
murder
moving
cars
walkout
tactics
green
anger
many
conduct
prosecuted
welcome
vice
impartial
depots
three
politics
keep
force
booklet
looking
magic
audience
respect
judge
thank
you
telephone
wasting
aims
delinquent
average
afraid
feed
I'd
foul
page

affecting
code
question
auditorium
split
hardly
energy
responsibility
satellites
nation
prophesy
forewarn
overmatched
possible
legal
plank
relief
dictate
plate
congested
ring
law making body
fool
following
again
publicity
licenses
side by side
open
inj**us**tices
white collar
engineering
fleeting
listen
entire
associate
disperse
activity
attractive
operator
during
whose
gratitude
fortunately
Goforth
season
disciplinary
prior
rapists
work
touchstone
drifted
waited
legislature
done
act
soft
flagman
motion
concessions
youth
highway
dabbling
unity
food
morally
sustain
ordinances
enforcement
salesmen
did
thieves
Little League
Plato
matter
important
mule
unfairly
telegraph
neither
wonderful
that's
elected
declared
sneak
individuals
skimpily
solidly
pushing
learned
stenographers
forgotten
trained
garden
presence
forgot
surprise
period
shaky
Tutwiler
investigation
outsiders
entertain
enroll
corner
John

something
University
captain
tolerate
rank
heat
enabling
above
reasons
old
one-yard
need
gain
all
docket
economical
rates
preserved
get
dispatch
audience
cross
creed
ticker
feelings
canine
outrageous
joyous
section
retail
engineer
mad
stands
feared
once
run
over
messing
stamps
statue
shoving
examiner
end
just
yelling
with
them
mistake
parking meter
forward
want
arrests
chairman
dynamite
lie detector
seconds
capacities
black belt
carry
states
jump
restaurants
state
action
picture
tried
frazzle
spared
growing
dear
healthy
anywhere
permission
Yankees
now
invitation
carpet
catch
death
sentiment
buttinskys
expenditures
chance
Magic Mineral Lodge
permanent
grabbing
weight
lewd
supervision
off
baseball
uniform
front
agitate
granted
least
check
throughout
brief
agencies
physician
bone
place
Sunday
lady officers
carnation
manner

rain hats
burner
radicals
statements
tears
maid
canal
closed
culprit
welfare
s.o.b.
there
stooges
relations
calling
stay
principles
afford
ties
stir
employees
both
rise
integrated
without
can
prayer
hard
running
history
bingo
fir
field
practice
wire
nothing
sea
go
fan
from
money
Mercury
pups
silent
risk
private
head
should
firms
usurping
teams
furnish
nature
sent
wrecking
insist
make
gone
silly
train
druggist
circulating
prejudged
mortgage
demand
the
House
packers
skyrocketed
journal
Congress
baby
cave
integration
natural
tie-ups
allow
alliance
hill
term
runaway
Southern Bell
plumbing
jealous
go-cart
window
denies
enter
damn
settlement
poke
speak
homes
satisfied
fraudulent
resentment
room
prosperous
order
receipt
enclose
brainwash
Commies
tip

desire
case
deep
backbiting
bicycle detail
slow
Naples
rink
hit
cowboys
itself
flagrant
flea
yapping
approximately
gradually
dumb
lawn
temper
same
long
distance
picketing
borne
self-explanatory
sign
merchant
going
Ohio
worried
paroling
year
slaughter
difference
underpasses
own
was
dim
statistical
fact
do
ascertain
collar
kingpin
fatalities
reading
advertise
pulpit
fleer
taken
hire
base
sailor
pennies
rat racing
engage
avoid
gullible
mine
loose
boar
partly
patrol
stuff
very
passed
interstate
name
family
our
plenty
since
delegates
air fields
and
give
sprinkler
liberties
we
straddle
ad valorem
muffler
pledge
impeach
plain-clothes
bums
contempt
conditions
because
examination
Gehrig
honorable
wrong
faithfully
out-of-towners
microphone
teacher
Orient
motor
fire alarm
occasionally
politicians
facing
motel
funeral

skimpy
crew
Studebaker
station wagon
might
petitions
application
pedestrian
quota
then
fire hydrants
he'd
governments
doing
wife
one
several
iota
jeopardized
enacted
success
doctors
dies
bond
tripled
earth
storm
meeting
uphold
arms
Angus
drop
violence
oath
impose
confederate
San Francisco
said
intend
four
auxiliary
civil
immediately
King
their
needs
band
authority
leaders
strike
release
anything
blight
spring
yield
bribe
entertainment
hotel
offer
shoes
racquet
approved
tree's
prices
runoff
rehabilitation
service
names
dawn
shut
tire
identity
comforting
short
only
balloons
whites
quicker
kid
boycott the devil
lack
lowest
stage
Mr. Pepper
powers
spin
his
yelled
regardless
turned
calculated
among
drinks
suitcase
skinny
pistol
cover
backwards
sort
button
approach
ocean
Lucille
sentence
inheritance

The Statement

June 11, 1963

Ladies and days,
we have enough rain
without any outside

whites collect
this black eye.

Sir, we need
the outside
to leave us knives
again
        and rocks.

Now Kiss the Word Lips on This Paper

I eat a piece of paper with the word *honey* written on it and give my son the word *toast* and he eats it whole. I cover the windows with the words *white sky*, *red brick*, and *7 AM*, though it still feels like night, so I write to the weak sunlight, *let us feel worthy of your love.* We do not feel worthy, bound in our clothes made of paper with *clean* written all over them. We go out into the streets with our sticky notes made of *fire* and stick them on everything. Nothing burns. I take a note to my son's teacher that says *help* and she gives it right back with her red ink covering mine. *Help.* On my forehead, I write, *What?* I write on the school walls, *I hate you words. You are not worthy of my love, anymore.* And the words are quiet. So, I say them out loud. I yell all the words I can yell. *Walnut! Suitcase! Pistol! Wastebasket!* I keep spitting words trying to rid them from my mouth.

Bull, Unseen

After a photograph by Colin Jones, May 3, 1963

Find *tar* in *star* in *start*, the night
fills my windows with tar
I don't want to see you anymore

look what you planted, black whiskers
on white cement, that harm still the boy
with his hand raised in a middle school

in our city that bled white, troubled.
The boy has something to say
but you did not leave us the words

to hear it. You keep arriving at every
crime scene carrying that stillborn belief
in your white heart, your chin, a moon

half-hidden in wet sand. What color
was the one good eye, forever now black
and white in the photograph, behind eyeglasses

that reflect not the trampled or the bound
but just the May clouds you look toward, a white
bull in each frame, charging at the other.

Black Ice

you are all in your desks
spread out in front of me
like another country's newspaper

someone draws an eye on loose-leaf
as a form of resistance
with eyeliner and tears

I try to break the hour
into pieces
too small for you to choke on

you look at your phone
as though it were a black well
into which you throw
the thoughts I want you to write

I should not place my hand
on your forehead
when you say you feel sick

you do not need more mothers
and I have enough sons

I wanted to be like a river to you,
something you could step into,
float on, but my offerings are more

like the glassy ice that holds
the grass down to the ground

I didn't want to do all the talking
I wanted to do the taking in

I need you to be suns, now,
and send me back to my source.

Peach Preserves

The window uploads another dawn:
a blanched sky etched
with the crooked tines of winter trees.

An hour ahead in a bigger city,
men are already being assholes.
Their daughters' white legs like

the throats of swans are just now
unfolding out of bedcovers,
little *no*s still developing

in their mouths, birds preparing
to fly from their middle fingers.
Their faces are painted over

the sisters who came before them
with fathers who woke early, footsteps loud
enough to be heard from another decade,

tied their ties and left for work. Time
to make another law to hold down the heat
like a nurse restrains a patient, love

left at home, a plant that knows
it can grow only in certain zones,
a girl born with fingers on white

keys, we see her in a still life
through a hole in the fence. A fine
wife holds down an armchair with her

heavenly body as her daughter sings
a song over the recording of a song,
before central air, when heat was

the great leveler, canned fish
on a cold plate. They drink tea from
the teapot inked on the blue bird.

Peachtree Circle

The lawn not repainted since the '60s.
A housedress with the same name

as the flowers in her front yard
grows back every day to check

the mail. Iris. Across the street,
two girls in swimsuits throw

sandwiches into the bushes,
the pattern of the iron furniture

repeated on the backs of their
legs. In the newspaper, an older sister

in a belle dress complains forever
on the back row of every photo.

The ink remembers the list
that girls had to be born onto.

All the papers were thrown out,
but the flight patterns of shuttlecocks

write the names, again, in the air
of the junior high gymnasium

that tries to be a grove. If there is
still a peach tree on the circle

the girls never think to ask. They raise
their hands to go to the restroom

when they don't really have to go.
They just want to get out of climbing

the rope, again, and the suicides.

The Headache

A headache wakes
before a woman
and touches the valuables
on her bedside table
leaving prints on the water
glass, then is gone
to the place where dogs
may go when they sleep
so she wonders, but then
the headache returns
and where is the dog?
She will read *The Lady*
with the Dog to understand
how a pain could
escape its white bottle
and be missed
and she will phone
the police to report
her need for a housedress
to be the woman
in a housedress
at lunchtime looking
for her headache
named after a season
of her childhood.
No dogs were harmed

in the making
of this headache, but
the woman may still
be aching even without
a head.

Play-by-Play

Shine threw to Billy
Billy threw to Piccolo Pete

Pete threw to Miles
who threw Joe out at home

Slim threw to Abe
who threw out the girl

and she came back again
then Shine threw her out

and she came back again
then Billy threw her out

so she never made it home.
What was thrown

was not seen clearly
from high up in the stands

or not seen at all though
it fit like a lady's

kneecap in Abe's hand.

A Finger Holds Down a Key

When there's fog in this city
streetlights at dawn up on the hill
get to be campfires at sundown
like the ones in books about war
where the soldiers settle in
for the night while a day's ride
away, ladies are being laced
into their party dresses,
but the party will only be
so much fun, knowing that soldiers
are blowing into their hands
feeling their deaths as close
as dance partners.
Then, the morning light pulls
the fog away like a boy
carrying his bedcovers
and the fires put themselves out
and a red bird scars the air

Forever Bull

I'm always afraid to come back to you
and stand at the fence of your white
pasture, white heat, white grass, white
flies. The only black is in the middle
of your one good eye. White Bull.

By now, I know what I can take
from you. I love your words torn apart
and tied up like colored flags.

From your white mud, you gave me wishbones,
black holes, hairpins, wave pools.
I stand by the waterfall we make together.
I'm going to say, I love you, now, because
you left the words to say it.
I love you, now.

I write you back into your pen
where you will always be. A flag
lets out a prayer over your white body,
                    when the wind.

Clemency

The rains come up from the gulf so heavy
this morning that the night will not release
the daylight and the blacked-out city
from a distance looks like a mountain painted
in grays just far away enough that we cannot see
its waterfall, or the path crooked as bleeding ink,
or the tree house with smoke and a wise man sitting
cross-legged, repeating the truths of yearbooks.

Where this mountain cuts into the sky,
we can see a break in the clouds,
and we know the rain will end, soon, taking
with it the man, the smoke, the little house,
the path, the waterfall, and the great mountain
and leave us with our city of wet boxes.
Viaducts cleaner but not clean.

The underside of a goose burns as it flies.
It carries something in its bill—a handle, a rope—
drawing closed the white heaven that's been hanging
over someone else's memories.

Sister City

I wish I had been left the words to go back and change
your beginning, or are you still beginning, are you
just being born? I was born inside of you, after
white kid gloves and before remote controls.

I was hidden in the hills cut from brown construction paper.
My favorite rooms were closets and books, sewn
into my dresses, hair rolled or feathered for church.
There's nothing I would change about my beginning,

but have I begun? I have loved a summer morning waiting
for a party better than I've loved any birthday, bicycling
around a quiet circle, safer than safe. There is nothing
I can say to change the feeling visitors get when they pass

through you. You are the pit bull at the fence that
people cross the street to avoid, they can't see the
church bells swinging from your belly. *Rib* in *terrible*,
they come to you for the ribs, to sit at the bar and eat

the fish that turns a body into a gulf. It's ok for us
to visit violence as though it were a neighbor's funeral.
We say we didn't know her, or not well, but we were family.
When we did not answer her calls, when we avoided her

at holiday parties, we were getting to know her better.
When I left home, you became one page in an old textbook,
and when I returned, after swearing I would never,
I could barely get through you with your numbered streets

trailing off like the paths of dropped coins. I wanted to make
something for strangers to love, for Virginia, Elizabeth,
Gertrude, Lucille. This song is not for any of them, though.
I made it for you, sister, because you sang it to me.

Jefferson Memorial Gardens

Theo Eugene Connor

All the Mays
you have lived
fly over your grave
this afternoon,
an aircraft pulls
an *of course*
across a gulf sky,
though we are far
from the gulf,
water oak.

Unreal flowers
drop their real colors
onto your name
in metal turned
lake green, you may
be swimming
under the skin of the land,
you may be alive
again in the form
of a fat lamb, a black
snake, a bull
horn, a traffic jam.
How would I know?

You may have come back
as me.

From way up above,
we must appear to be
the same thing.
Beyond a border of trees,
police officers
run practice drills,
bullets in the air
where bird notes
used to be.

You really left me
nothing. You did not
know that I would exist,
but you made a war
for me anyway

to have what I did
not earn. We remain
on separate sides
of the same side
of something as flat
as the moon
in a drawing
of the moon.

Acknowledgments

Thank you to the editors who first published versions of these poems:

Bennington Review: "I Was Misty," "Matinee"

The Hunger: "A Promise for the Egg Filled with Cotton Balls,"
"Peach Preserves"

Ilanot Review: "Bricking Up the Windows," "Stop Breathing"

The Louisville Review: "The Papers of Bull Connor," "The
Belongings," "A Finger Holds Down a Key," "Forever Bull"

Open Letters Monthly: "Bull in Office"

Public Pool: "Choke Pear," "The Davids"

Spoon River Poetry Review: "A Call to Arms," "Another Garden
Crusade"

SWWIM: "Now Kiss the Word Lips on This Paper"

Tinderbox: "Heave in Heaven"

The title of the poem "I Became a Postcard of Myself" is a line taken from the film *One Sings, the Other Doesn't* by Agnès Varda (Ciné-tamaris, 1977).

"The Statement" is an erasure of Bull Connor's public statement in response to President Kennedy's decision to send federal troops to Birmingham in the summer of 1963.

I am very thankful for the support of the National Endowment for the Arts, the Sustainable Arts Foundation, and the Crosstown Arts Residency Program. This book took nearly a decade to make its way into the world. During those years, I had young children at home and taught poetry in public schools. There were long spells when I felt far away from this work.

Every time I received a grant or fellowship, I was drawn back in and given the time and space I needed to write. I hope many more artists can receive that kind of support when they need it most.

Thank you to the staff of the Birmingham Public Library, especially the librarians at the Avondale and Central branches. Most of the words used in these poems were pulled from the library's archives and its digital collection of the Theophilus Eugene "Bull" Connor Papers, 1959–1963. I also used words found in *Carry Me Home*, by Diane McWhorter, and *Bull Connor*, by William A. Nunnelley.

To Sarah, Emma, Danika, Alban, Joanna, and the whole Sarabande team, thank you for giving this book such careful attention. Thank you to my DISCO family for filling my life with art and words. Thank you, Jim, for the conversation in our parents' kitchen that led to this book. Thank you, Kristin Bock and Michael Robins, for reading early versions of these poems and giving encouragement when I did not know how far I had to go. Thank you, Katie Rogers, for visiting the cemetery with me. Thank you, Andrea Dapkus, for showing me how to look for the golden light. Thank you, Jan, for being such a great mother and friend. I love you, Angus and Nicholas. And to Chip, my first reader and very best friend, I am so lucky to share this life with you.

ANDREA DAPKUS

ELIZABETH HUGHEY is the author of *Sunday Houses the Sunday House* (University of Iowa Press), and *Guest Host* (The National Poetry Review Press). She has received fellowships from the National Endowment for the Arts and the Sustainable Arts Foundation. She is the co-founder and Programming Director of the Desert Island Supply Co. (DISCO), a literary arts center in Birmingham, Alabama. She is the 2020 winner of the Kathryn A. Morton Prize in Poetry, chosen by Alberto Ríos.

SARABANDE BOOKS is a nonprofit literary press located in Lousiville, KY. Founded in 1994 to champion poetry, short fiction, and essay, we are committed to creating lasting editions that honor exceptional writing. For more information, please visit sarabandebooks.org.